PARAGRAPH WRITING AND EDITING

WORKBOOK FOR HIGH SCHOOL

A PARAGRAPH WRITING WORKBOOK FOR TEENS GUIDING THEM HOW TO WRITE AN AWESOME PARAGRAPH

MW00882016

DR. FANATOMY
★★★★★

copyright@ dr. fanatomy 2024

All rights reserved. No part of this publication may be reproduced, distributed, or transmitted in any form or by any means, including photocopying, recording, or other electronic or mechanical methods, without the prior written permission of the publisher, except in the case of brief quotations embodied in critical reviews and certain other noncommercial uses permitted by copyright law.

This book is a work of non-fiction, and any resemblance to actual persons, living or dead, or actual events is purely coincidental.

The information and techniques described in this book are intended for educational and informational purposes only. The author and publisher shall not be held liable for any injury, damage, or loss arising from using or misusing the information presented in this book.

While every effort has been made to ensure the accuracy of the information contained within this book, the author and publisher make no warranties or representations express or implied, about the completeness, accuracy, reliability, suitability, or availability with respect to the contents of this book for any purpose. The use of any information provided in this book is at the reader's own risk.

DR. FANATOMY

BONUS BOOKLET FOR YOU!

With great pleasure, I warmly welcome you to purchase the book. Congratulations on stepping towards improving yourself and developing the skills necessary to thrive as a teenager and beyond.

Below is a surprise gift for you!

Download it from the link (or scan the QR code below)
https://bit.ly/TeeNavigationBonus

TABLE OF CONTENTS

1. Introduction to Paragraph Editing

Welcome Message

Welcome to the exciting world of paragraph editing! This chapter will explore the secrets behind crafting clear, cohesive, and impactful paragraphs. But before we dive into the nitty-gritty of editing, let's take a moment to understand why mastering paragraph editing is so essential for becoming a skilled writer.

So, are you ready to embark on this adventure with me?

Understanding the Importance of Paragraph Editing:

Picture this: You're at a concert, waiting for your favorite band to appear. The first note echoes through the venue, the lights dim, and the crowd goes wild with excitement. But instead of a beautiful melody, you're met with a jumbled mess of sounds that leave you confused and overwhelmed—just like a poorly written paragraph can leave your readers feeling lost and frustrated.

That's where paragraph editing comes in - it's like the conductor of your writing, ensuring each sentence flows smoothly into the next. It helps your ideas come across clearly and precisely, guiding your readers through your thoughts like a gentle breeze. Whether you're writing an essay, a story, or a report, mastering paragraph editing is crucial for keeping your audience engaged and getting your message across effectively.

The Role of Clear and Cohesive Paragraphs in Effective Writing:

Hey there! Think of paragraphs as the building blocks that hold your work together when writing. They're like the foundation of a house, giving your composition a solid backbone. Each paragraph is a self-contained piece that revolves around a central idea, supported by relevant details and examples.

To help you understand this better, let's use an analogy. Think of your writing as a road trip and each paragraph as a unique destination. Like road signs guide travelers from one place to the next, well-structured paragraphs guide your readers from one idea to the next.

With some proper editing, your writing journey will stay on track, and your audience will understand what you're saying clearly and concisely.

Common Mistakes in Paragraph Structure:

Let's face it – we all make mistakes when writing paragraphs. From using long sentences to disjointed ideas, we've all been there. These errors can be frustrating and make even the best writers feel like they're not progressing.

One common mistake is creating a "wall of text." Do you know the paragraphs that are just words strung together with no breaks? They can be challenging to read, and sometimes, they might even make you feel suffocating!

Another common mistake is forgetting to include a clear and concise topic sentence. Think of it as the GPS for your paragraph. Without it, your paragraph might feel like a lost puppy wandering without direction.

But don't worry! I'm here to help you conquer these common paragraph pitfalls and become a master of your craft.

So, get ready to learn more about paragraph editing. With some practice and creativity, you'll soon be crafting clear, cohesive, and captivating paragraphs. Your readers will be hooked from the first sentence!

Examples of some Common Errors

Run-on sentences occur when two or more independent clauses are improperly joined without appropriate punctuation or conjunctions.

For example: *"I went to the store and bought some groceries."*

The independent clauses should be separated by a period or conjunction like "and" or "but.

A lack of a **topic sentence** results in paragraphs needing more focus and coherence.

For instance, in a paragraph about the benefits of exercise, a clear topic sentence could be: *"Regular exercise offers numerous health benefits, including improved cardiovascular health and reduced risk of chronic diseases."*

Weak transitions or the absence of transitions can lead to abrupt shifts between sentences, disrupting the flow of the paragraph.

Example: *"She loved reading books. She spent hours at the library."* Adding a transition such as *"Additionally"* would improve the flow: *"Additionally, she spent hours at the library."*

Paragraphs must have **supporting details** to feel supported. For instance, in a paragraph discussing climate change, providing specific examples of its effects, *such as rising sea levels and extreme weather events, strengthens the argument and engages the reader.*

Inconsistent tone or style undermines the coherence of paragraphs. For example, a paragraph that *begins with a formal tone and transitions abruptly to a casual tone can confuse readers and diminish the impact of the message.*

TRIVIA CORNER

Did you know that some of the world's most beloved stories had difficulty getting published?

Take J.K. Rowling and her Harry Potter series, for example. Rowling faced rejection from multiple publishers before finally getting her big break. But she didn't give up, and her magical world eventually captured the hearts of millions of readers worldwide. This story reminds us that even the most successful writers face challenges, but they never give up.

So, if you ever feel discouraged in your writing, remember that perseverance is the key to success!

ACTIVITY CORNER 1

Error Identification Exercise

Edit the provided paragraph to identify and correct grammar, spelling, or punctuation errors. Explain the errors you found and the corrections you made.

Paragraph 1: Is Social Media Making You Sad *(with Errors)*:

Social media has become an undeniable force in our lives. With millions of users worldwide, it allows us to connect with friends and family, share experiences, and stay informed about current events. But there's a flip side to this coin. Social media can be a breeding ground for negativity and unrealistic expectations. Many users present a curated version of their lives, showcasing only the highlight reels. This can lead to feelings of inadequacy and envy amongst others, especially teenagers who are still developing their self-esteem.

Paragraph 2: The Future of Jobs *(with Errors):*

With automation rapidly taking over many tasks, high schoolers today face a unique challenge: what jobs will even exist by the time they graduate? This uncertainty can be stressful, leading to feelings of confusion and a lack of direction when choosing a career path. The good news is, the future of work isn't all doom and gloom! New job opportunities are constantly emerging, especially in fields that require creativity, critical thinking, and the ability to adapt to change. By focusing on developing these skills, high schoolers can prepare themselves for a successful future, regardless of the specific job title they may hold.

2. The Anatomy of a Paragraph

Understanding the Basics

Effective writing requires well-crafted paragraphs, which are cohesive units of thought that convey a single idea or argument. To communicate ideas clearly and persuasively, it is essential to understand the structure of a paragraph. In this chapter, we will examine the different parts of a paragraph, learn about its key components, and analyze its structure.

Example Paragraph:

"The internet has revolutionized the way we communicate and access information. With just a few clicks, we can connect with friends across the globe, conduct research on any topic imaginable, and stay informed about current events. However, this unprecedented access to information raises concerns about privacy and misinformation. Despite these challenges, the internet remains a powerful tool for personal and professional endeavors."

Components of a Well-Structured Paragraph

Did you know that a well-written paragraph has three essential parts?

First, it starts with a topic sentence that tells the reader about the paragraph. Then, it has supporting details that explain or prove the topic sentence. Finally, it ends with a concluding sentence that summarizes the main point. Hope that helps!

Topic Sentence: The topic sentence serves as the backbone of the paragraph, expressing the main idea or argument. It focuses on the paragraph and sets the tone for the discussion.

For example, in our sample paragraph, the topic sentence is: *"The internet has revolutionized the way we communicate and access information."*

Supporting Details: Supporting details provide evidence, examples, or explanations that strengthen and develop the main idea presented in the topic sentence. These details should be relevant and compelling, offering further insight.

In our example paragraph, supporting details include statistics on Internet usage, personal anecdotes about the benefits of online communication, or examples of how the Internet has transformed industries.

Concluding Sentence: The concluding sentence summarizes the main points, reinforces the significance of the main idea, and transitions smoothly to the next paragraph, providing closure.

In conclusion, the internet is a valuable resource but also a source of concern. *"Despite these Internets, the Internet remains a powerful tool for personal and professional endeavors."*

Identifying and Analyzing Paragraph Structure

Once you comprehend the elements of a well-structured paragraph, you can analyze paragraphs to determine their structure and effectiveness.

Identifying Structure: When examining the structure of a paragraph, it is essential to locate a concise topic sentence that highlights the main idea.

Supporting details should then be provided to expand the topic sentence and add depth to the paragraph. Lastly, a concluding sentence summarizing the main points should be included to tie everything together. It is important to note how each component contributes to the overall coherence and persuasiveness of the paragraph.

Analyzing Effectiveness: Please evaluate the paragraph's effectiveness by assessing how well it communicates its main idea, the relevance and strength of the supporting details, and the clarity and coherence of the writing.

Reflect on whether the paragraph achieves its intended purpose and engages the reader effectively. Please ensure to correct any spelling, grammar, and punctuation errors.

Practice Exercises on Identifying Paragraph Components

Practice exercises allow you to apply your knowledge of paragraph structure and analysis.

Exercise: Read a series of paragraphs and identify the topic sentence, supporting details, and concluding sentence in each one. Consider how these components work together to convey the paragraph's main idea.

Solution: Compare your analysis with provided solutions to gain insights into practical paragraph construction and refine your analytical skills.

By mastering the anatomy of a paragraph and honing your skills in identifying and analyzing paragraph structure, you'll become a more confident and proficient writer, capable of crafting compelling and persuasive prose.

TRIVIA CORNER

- *Did you know that the longest English sentence ever published contains 13,955 words? It's found in Jonathan Coe's novel "The Rotter's Club" and is a testament to the versatility and flexibility of sentence structure in writing.*

- *The shortest paragraph is attributed to Edgar Allan Poe's story "A Descent into the Maelström." It consists of just one word: "Yes!" This demonstrates that even a single word can convey profound meaning within a narrative context.*

- *Mark Twain famously quipped, "I didn't have time to write a short letter, so I wrote a long one instead." This humorous observation underscores the challenge of crafting concise and compelling writing, where brevity often requires more effort than verbosity.*

- *In professional typesetting, the first line of a paragraph is often indented to visually separate it from the preceding text. This tradition dates back to the era of manual typesetting when typographers used physical pieces of metal to space out text and improve readability.*

ACTIVITY CORNER 2

Activity Exercise: Anatomy of a Paragraph

Objective:

This activity aims to reinforce understanding of the components of a well-structured paragraph and practice identifying and analyzing paragraph structure.

Instructions:

Paragraph Analysis: Below are 2 sample paragraphs. Analyze the paragraph and identify the following components:

- Topic sentence
- Supporting details
- Concluding sentence (if applicable)

Discussion and Reflection: After analyzing the paragraph, reflect on how each component contributes to the overall effectiveness of the paragraph. Consider the clarity, coherence, and persuasiveness of the writing.

Peer Review Activity: Discuss your analysis with a peer. Exchange paragraphs you have written independently and provide constructive feedback to help improve each other's writing.

Paragraph Reconstruction Challenge: Rearrange the sentences below to create a clear and cohesive paragraph. Consider how each sentence contributes to the overall flow and meaning of the paragraph.

Peer Evaluation: Compare your analysis and paragraph reconstruction with the solution sheet. Reflect on areas for improvement and discuss with your peers.

ACTIVITY CORNER 2

Paragraph 1: Exploring the Cosmos

"The exploration of space has always fascinated humankind. From the first glimpse of the moon through telescopes to the landing of rovers on distant planets, humans have been driven by a desire to understand the universe beyond Earth. With advancements in technology, space exploration has reached new heights, allowing us to probe the depths of our solar system and beyond. However, space exploration is not without its challenges. Astronauts face numerous risks, from exposure to cosmic radiation to the psychological effects of long-duration space travel. Despite these challenges, the quest for knowledge and discovery continues to fuel our exploration of the final frontier."

Paragraph 2: Confronting Climate Change

"The threat of climate change looms large over our planet, casting a shadow of uncertainty over the future of our ecosystems. The warming of Earth's atmosphere has triggered a cascade of environmental impacts, from the melting of polar ice caps to the intensification of extreme weather events. Hurricanes, wildfires, and droughts have become increasingly frequent and severe, wreaking havoc on communities and habitats worldwide. Agriculture and food security are also under threat, as shifting weather patterns disrupt growing seasons and threaten crop yields. Urgent action is needed to address the root causes of climate change and safeguard the health and stability of our planet for generations to come."

14

3. Transition Words and Phrases

Welcome to Chapter 3 of "Paragraph Writing for High School: A Teen Writer's Workbook."

In this chapter, we will discuss the significance of using transition words and phrases in writing well-structured and logical paragraphs. We will examine the different roles of transitions and offer examples to help you understand how to use them effectively.

Understanding the Function of Transitions in Paragraphs

Transition words and phrases are crucial tools in guiding readers through writing. They connect ideas, show relationships between sentences and paragraphs, and improve overall flow.

Example:

Paragraph without Transitions:

"I enjoy hiking. I often go to the nearby trails. The scenery is beautiful. I feel peaceful when surrounded by nature."

Paragraph with Transitions:

"I enjoy hiking because it allows me to connect with nature. Additionally, I often go to the nearby trails, where the scenery is beautiful. As a result, I feel peaceful and rejuvenated after spending time outdoors."

In the second paragraph, the use of transitions such as "because," "additionally," and "as a result" helps to connect the ideas more smoothly and **logically, creating a more coherent narrative.**

Classification of Transition words

Transition words and phrases can be classified into different types based on their functions. These include but are not limited to addition, contrast, cause and effect, time sequence, and illustration.

Example:

- *Addition*: Furthermore, Moreover, Additionally
- *Contrast*: However, On the other hand, Conversely
- *Cause and Effect*: Consequently, Therefore, Thus
- *Time Sequence*: Meanwhile, Next, Finally
- *Illustration*: For example, Specifically, In other words

Practice exercises allow you to incorporate transition words and phrases into your writing effectively.

Example Exercise:

Add appropriate transition words or phrases to the following paragraph to improve coherence and flow:

"Studying for exams can be challenging. You need to manage your time effectively, review your notes regularly, and stay focused during study sessions."

Solution:

"Studying for exams can be challenging. However, by managing your time effectively, you can alleviate some of the stress. Additionally, reviewing your notes regularly is crucial to reinforce your understanding of the material. Moreover, staying focused during study sessions will maximize your productivity and retention."

By mastering the use of transition words and phrases, you'll enhance the clarity and coherence of your writing, making it more engaging and accessible for your readers—practice incorporating transitions into your paragraphs to improve your writing skills further.

◎ ACTIVITY CORNER 3

Exercise 1: Identifying and Correcting Transitions
Instructions:

Read the following paragraphs and identify the missing transitions. Then, fill in the blanks with appropriate transition words or phrases to improve the coherence and flow of the paragraphs.

Paragraph 1:

(1) I love spending time outdoors. (2) I often go for long walks in the park. (3) The fresh air and greenery help me relax. (4) My favorite spot is the lake. (5) It's surrounded by tall trees. (6) There, I can sit and read for hours. (7) I feel a sense of peace by the water.

Paragraph 2:

(1) I enjoy experimenting in the kitchen. (2) I like trying out new recipes. (3) Cooking allows me to express my creativity. (4) However, sometimes things don't turn out as expected. (5) This can be frustrating. (6) I've learned to laugh off culinary mishaps. (7) It's all part of the learning process.

Paragraph 3:

(1) I woke up early in the morning. (2) I hurriedly got dressed. (3) I had an important meeting to attend. (4) I left the house without having breakfast. (5) I caught the bus just in time. (6) I arrived at the office feeling anxious.

Paragraph 4:

(1) My cat is a mischievous little creature. (2) She often gets into trouble. (3) She knocked over a vase yesterday. (4) She didn't seem to realize what she'd done. (5) She continued to play as if nothing had happened. (6) She's always keeping me on my toes.

18

4. Sentence Variety and Clarity

Welcome to Chapter 4 of "Paragraph Writing for High School: A Teen Writer's Workbook." In this chapter, we will discuss the importance of having a variety of sentences and making them clear to improve the overall coherence and effectiveness of your writing. We will provide strategies and techniques to achieve sentence variety and clarity and engaging practice exercises to help you sharpen your skills.

Importance of Sentence Variety for Paragraph Coherence:

Sentence variety is crucial in maintaining reader engagement and ensuring paragraph coherence. Using a variety of sentence lengths, structures, and types can prevent your writing from becoming monotonous and predictable.

Example:

Consider the following paragraph with a repetitive sentence structure:

"I woke up early. I had breakfast. I went to school. I attended classes. I came home."

Now, observe how sentence variety enhances the paragraph's coherence:

"In the early morning light, I awoke to the chirping of birds. After savoring a hearty breakfast, I embarked on my journey to school. I immersed myself in various classes throughout the day, eagerly absorbing new knowledge. As the day drew close, I returned home, reflecting on the day's adventures."

Strategies for Achieving Sentence Variety :

Achieving sentence variety involves varying sentence length, structure, and type. You can create a more dynamic and engaging narrative by incorporating different sentence constructions.

Example:

Varying Sentence Length: Combine short and long sentences to create rhythm and emphasis.

"She ran as fast as her legs could carry her, her heart pounding."

Varying Sentence Structure: Experiment with sentence structures, including simple, compound, and complex sentences.

"The sun rose, casting a warm glow over the landscape, and the birds began their morning serenade."

Varying Sentence Type: Use declarative, interrogative, imperative, and exclamatory sentences to convey different tones and moods.

"He walked along the deserted beach, lost in thought. (declarative)"

"Have you ever danced in the rain? (interrogative)"

"Close your eyes and make a wish. (imperative)"

"What a beautiful sight! (exclamatory)"

Techniques for Achieving Clarity and Conciseness in Sentences

Effective communication requires clear and concise sentences. Avoid wordiness and ambiguity to ensure your message is conveyed clearly.

Example:

Eliminate Redundancy: Remove unnecessary words or phrases that repeat information.

"The large, big tree stood tall in the center of the park." (redundant)

"The large tree stood tall in the center of the park." (concise)

Use Specific Language: Replace vague or general terms with precise and descriptive language.

"She walked into the room with something in her hand." (vague)

"She entered the room holding a bouquet of flowers." (specific)

Practice Exercises on Sentence Variety and Clarity

Practice exercises allow you to apply the strategies and techniques learned to improve your writing skills.

Example Exercise:

Revise the following sentence to improve clarity and conciseness:

"I couldn't attend the party because I had a lot of homework to finish."

Solution:

"I couldn't attend the party because I had a lot of homework to finish."

By mastering sentence variety and clarity, you'll enhance the readability and impact of your writing, captivating your readers and effectively conveying your ideas. So, let's dive into the practice exercises and refine your skills!

TRIVIA CORNER

- **Emoji Evolution**: *Did you know that emojis can add variety to your writing? Originally created in Japan in the late 1990s, emojis have become a popular way to express emotions and ideas in digital communication. Incorporating emojis into your writing can add a fun and unique touch to your paragraphs.*

- **Dr. Seuss's Secret:** *The beloved children's author Dr. Seuss, known for his whimsical stories and playful rhymes, was a master of sentence variety. He used short, snappy sentences alongside long, elaborate ones to create rhythm and flow in his books like "The Cat in the Hat" and "Green Eggs and Ham."*

◎ ACTIVITY CORNER 4
Activity: Sentence Shuffle

Activity 1 Prompt:

1. Provide students with a paragraph that lacks sentence variety.
2. Ask them to rearrange the sentences to create a more engaging and varied paragraph.

Paragraph 1 :

"The sun was shining brightly in the sky. The birds were singing happily in the trees. I went for a walk in the park. The flowers were blooming beautifully in the garden. It was a lovely day."

Activity 2 Prompt:

1. Provide students with a paragraph that lacks clarity and conciseness.
2. Ask them to revise the paragraph to make it clearer and more concise.

Paragraph 2 :

"I have a friend who lives in a house that is big and yellow and has a garden with lots of flowers in it. We sometimes go there to play and have fun."

Activity 3 Prompt:

1. Provide students with a paragraph containing repetitive sentence structures.
2. Ask them to transform the sentences to create a more varied and engaging paragraph.

Paragraph 3 : "I woke up early in the morning. I brushed my teeth. I ate breakfast. I walked to school. I met my friends. I attended classes. I came back home. I did my homework. I went to bed."

5. Editing for Unity and Coherence

Editing for Unity and Coherence

Welcome to Chapter 5 of "Paragraph Editing For High School: A Teen Writer's Workbook"! In this chapter, we'll explore how to polish your paragraphs to ensure they flow smoothly and convey your ideas effectively.

Understanding Unity and Coherence in Paragraphs:

Unity and coherence are two essential elements of effective writing. Unity ensures that all sentences in a paragraph are centered around a central idea or theme, while coherence ensures logical connections between sentences. It's like building a puzzle, where each piece (sentence) fits together to form a complete picture (paragraph).

For instance, if you're writing about the advantages of exercising, all sentences should emphasize different aspects of exercise, such as physical health, mental well-being, or social interaction.

Identifying and Correcting Paragraphs Lacking Unity or Coherence:

Unity and coherence are two essential elements of effective writing. Unity ensures that all sentences in a paragraph are centered around a central idea or theme, while coherence ensures logical connections between sentences. It's like building a puzzle, where each piece (sentence) fits together to form a complete picture (paragraph). For instance, if you're writing about the advantages of exercising, all sentences should emphasize different aspects of exercise, such as physical health, mental well-being, or social interaction.

Techniques for Ensuring Smooth Transitions and Logical Flow Between Sentences:

Creating smooth transitions in writing is crucial as it helps to connect sentences, guiding readers from one idea to another. Transition words and phrases, such as "however," "meanwhile," and "in conclusion," indicate shifts in thought and aid in maintaining coherence. Additionally, repeating significant words or using pronouns can reinforce connections between sentences

For instance, in a paragraph about climate change, pronouns like "it" or "this issue" can refer back to previously mentioned environmental concerns.

Practice Exercises on Editing for Unity and Coherence:

The exercises will help you practice identifying paragraphs that lack unity or coherence and making revisions to improve their clarity and cohesion. For instance, you may be asked to edit a paragraph about time management, ensuring that all sentences focus on strategies for prioritizing tasks and avoiding procrastination. By actively engaging with these exercises, you'll improve your editing skills and develop a knack for crafting well-structured paragraphs.

Example Paragraph and Revision:

Original Paragraph:

"I love spending time outdoors. My favorite activity is hiking in the mountains. I also enjoy swimming in the ocean. Another hobby of mine is gardening. Playing sports is fun, too."

Revised Paragraph:

"I love spending time outdoors, engaging in various activities that bring me joy. Hiking in the mountains allows me to connect with nature and challenge myself physically. Swimming in the ocean brings a sense of freedom and serenity as I glide through the waves. Gardening provides a peaceful escape, nurturing plants and watching them thrive. Additionally, playing sports with friends fosters camaraderie and healthy competition, adding excitement to my outdoor adventures."

Difference:

The original paragraph consists of fragmented sentences listing outdoor activities without a clear connection. The sentences are restructured and expanded in the revised paragraph to provide specific details and insights into each activity. Transition phrases like "Additionally" and "allows me to" are used to create coherence and ensure a smooth flow between ideas. As a result, the revised paragraph presents a unified and coherent narrative of the writer's outdoor experiences.

TRIVIA CORNER

- *Harry Potter and the Editor's Magic: Did you know that J.K. Rowling's famous "Harry Potter" series underwent extensive editing to ensure unity and coherence? Rowling worked closely with her editors to revise and refine the manuscripts, ensuring that each book maintained a seamless flow of storytelling while preserving the magical world of Hogwarts.*

- *The Power of Pixar's Storytelling: Pixar movies are renowned for their compelling narratives and emotional depth. Behind the scenes, Pixar's team of writers and editors meticulously craft each storyline, focusing on unity and coherence to engage audiences of all ages. From "Toy Story" to "Finding Nemo," every Pixar film undergoes rigorous editing to ensure a cohesive and impactful storytelling experience.*

- *The Evolution of Editing Software: In today's digital age, editing tools like Grammarly and Hemingway Editor have revolutionized the editing process. These software programs not only correct grammar and punctuation but also analyze the overall coherence and clarity of writing. High schoolers can utilize these tools to enhance their writing, ensuring their paragraphs are cohesive and well-structured.*

◎ ACTIVITY CORNER 5

Unity and Coherence Quiz:

Exercise:

Below are three paragraphs. Identify the paragraphs that lack unity or coherence and explain why. Then, revise the paragraphs to improve their unity and coherence. Provide explanations for each change.

Paragraph 1: "I woke up early in the morning. The sun was shining brightly outside. I had breakfast with my family. Then, I went for a walk in the park. I saw some birds chirping in the trees. It was a beautiful day."

Paragraph 2: "My favorite hobbies are reading, playing basketball, and painting. Reading allows me to relax and escape into different worlds. Playing basketball helps me stay active and socialize with friends. Painting allows me to express my creativity and emotions."

Paragraph 3: "I want to travel the world someday. There are so many places I want to visit. I want to see the Eiffel Tower in Paris, the Great Wall of China, and the beaches of Hawaii. Traveling allows me to experience new cultures and broaden my horizons."

Paragraph Puzzle Challenge:

Question:

Below are five jumbled sentences. Rearrange the sentences to create a unified and coherent paragraph about a day at the beach.

- *We spread out our beach towels and set up an umbrella for shade.*
- *The waves crashed against the shore, creating a soothing sound.*
- *After swimming and playing games, we enjoyed a picnic lunch on the sand.*
- *Children built sandcastles while adults relaxed and soaked up the sun.*
- *Seagulls soared overhead, searching for scraps of food.*

Matching Activity: Matching Paragraph Types

Instructions:

Match each paragraph with its corresponding type based on the characteristics of unity and coherence.

Paragraphs:

- *"I woke up early and had breakfast with my family. Afterward, I enjoyed a refreshing walk in the park, listening to the birds chirping in the trees under the bright morning sun."*

- *"My favorite hobbies are reading, playing basketball, and painting. Reading allows me to relax and escape into different worlds. Playing basketball helps me stay active and socialize with friends. Painting allows me to express my creativity and emotions."*

- *"One destination at the top of my travel bucket list is Paris, where I dream of seeing the iconic Eiffel Tower. Exploring famous landmarks like the Great Wall of China and relaxing on the beautiful beaches of Hawaii are also high on my list. Traveling allows me to immerse myself in new cultures and broaden my horizons."*

Paragraph Types:

A. Expository B. Narrative C. Descriptive

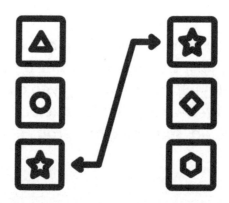

6. Polishing Paragraphs for Style and Tone

This chapter will explore the intricacies of style and tone in writing. As a high school student, you already possess excellent communication skills. However, honing your ability to craft well-structured paragraphs with precision can take your writing to new heights of sophistication and effectiveness.

Recognizing Different Writing Styles and Tones:

Consider the scenario of reading a news article about a recent scientific discovery. The text is likely to be formal, objective, and informative, which is typical of journalistic writing. This style is suitable for conveying factual information and maintaining a serious tone. Imagine a blog post discussing the same topic but from a personal perspective. The text will likely be written in a conversational, subjective, and expressive style, which is more casual and reflective. We can appreciate how authors adjust their style and tone to suit their intended audience by noticing these differences.

Example:

Please take a moment to consider the following two paragraphs discussing climate change. The first paragraph uses a formal approach and a severe tone to present statistical data and scientific evidence to support its arguments. In contrast, the second paragraph takes a conversational style and an empathetic tone to share personal anecdotes and emotional responses that convey the urgency of addressing climate change.

Adapting Style and Tone to Suit the Purpose and Audience of Writing:

Consider how the purpose and audience of our writing influence our style and tone. Suppose you must write a research paper for your science class; your audience is your teacher. Your teacher expects a formal tone and an objective presentation of facts. In this case, you should adopt a scholarly style and an informative tone to meet your audience's expectations and fulfill the assignment's requirements.

Example:

The purpose and audience of a letter to your best friend differ from those of a formal letter. You can use a more relaxed style and a personal tone that reflects your friend's interests and personality. Share stories and inside jokes, and use informal language that would resonate with your friend.

Strategies for Enhancing Writing Style and Tone in Paragraphs:

Now that we better understand the significance of style and tone in writing, let's explore some strategies to help us enhance them. One of the most effective strategies is using descriptive language and vivid imagery to engage the reader's senses and evoke emotions. By painting a clear picture with words, we can immerse our readers in the writing world and create a memorable experience.

Example:

Instead of saying, "The sunset was beautiful," we can enrich our description by saying, "The fiery hues of the setting sun painted the sky in shades of crimson and gold, casting a warm glow over the tranquil landscape." This descriptive language enhances our writing style and sets the tone by evoking feelings of awe and appreciation.

Practice Exercises on Polishing Paragraphs for Style and Tone:

Let's improve our understanding by putting these concepts into practice. We will refine paragraphs to achieve the desired style and tone. Engaging in hands-on exercises will enhance our skills and develop an intuition for crafting paragraphs that resonate with readers.

Example:

Based on a paragraph describing a busy city street, we will practice different writing styles and tones to evoke various moods and impressions. We might use a descriptive and nostalgic tone to capture the charm of a bygone era or choose a minimalist style and a detached tone to convey the anonymity of urban life.

We can become more versatile and expressive writers by refining our ability to polish paragraphs for style and tone. This will enable us to engage and captivate our audience with every word we write. So, let's jump in and discover the limitless potential of polished prose!

Original Paragraph: *"The forest was dark and eerie. The trees loomed overhead, casting long shadows on the forest floor. I felt a sense of unease as I ventured deeper into the woods. Suddenly, a twig snapped behind me, and I froze in fear."*

Step-by-Step Implementation of Polishing Style and Tone:

Recognizing Different Writing Styles and Tones:

- Identify the current style and tone: The paragraph has a descriptive style and a suspenseful tone, suitable for a mystery or horror story.
- Consider alternative styles and tones: We could explore shifting the style to be more poetic or the tone to be more introspective.

Adapting Style and Tone to Suit the Purpose and Audience:

- Determine the purpose and audience: If the purpose is to entertain a young adult audience, we can maintain the suspenseful tone but make the language more accessible and engaging.

- Adjust style and tone accordingly. We can infuse the paragraph with vivid imagery and a sense of urgency to captivate the reader's attention.

Strategies for Enhancing Writing Style and Tone:

- Incorporate descriptive language: Add sensory details to immerse the reader in the setting. For example, "The forest enveloped me in its cool embrace, the rustle of leaves like whispers in the wind." 33

- Adjust sentence structure: Vary sentence lengths and structures to create rhythm and flow. For instance, "Silence enveloped the forest. Shadows danced between the trees, their gnarled branches reaching for the sky."

Practice Exercises on Polishing Paragraphs for Style and Tone:

- Write the paragraph in a different style and tone. Experiment with a more poetic and reflective tone. For example, "In the forest's heart, shadows danced beneath the moon's gentle gaze. Each step I took echoed through the silent trees, a symphony of solitude."

Revised Paragraph:

"In the forest's heart, shadows danced beneath the moon's gentle gaze. Each step I took echoed through the silent trees, a symphony of solitude. The cool embrace of the woods enveloped me, every rustle of leaves a whisper in the wind. Lost in thought, I ventured deeper, the forest unfolding its secrets with each passing moment."

By following these steps, we can transform the original paragraph into a more engaging and evocative piece of writing, showcasing the importance of style and tone in crafting compelling prose.

TRIVIA CORNER

Did you know that famous author J.K. Rowling, best known for the Harry Potter series, wrote the first draft of "Harry Potter and the Philosopher's Stone" in longhand on a series of notepads?

She carefully crafted each paragraph, paying close attention to style and tone, before typing it on a typewriter. This meticulous approach highlights the importance of polishing paragraphs for style and tone, even for seasoned authors.

ACTIVITY CORNER 6

Activity 1: Style and Tone Analysis

Instructions: Provide students with paragraphs written in different styles and tones. Ask them to identify the style and tone of each paragraph and select the most appropriate option from the given choices.

Sample Paragraphs:

1. *"The sun dipped below the horizon, casting a golden hue across the sky. As I walked along the beach, the gentle lapping of the waves echoed in my ears, a soothing melody that calmed my racing thoughts."*

2. *"In the heart of the bustling city, skyscrapers towered overhead, their steel frames glinting in the sunlight. Amidst the chaos of the streets, I found solace in the anonymity of the crowd, a silent observer in the urban jungle."*

3. *"The forest enveloped me in its cool embrace, the rustle of leaves like whispers in the wind. Each step I took echoed through the silent trees, a symphony of solitude."*

Tone Options:

A. Reflective
B. Detached
C. Introspective
D. Energetic

Activity 2 : Tone Matching Game

Instructions: Provide students with sentences or short paragraphs written in different tones. Ask them to match each sentence/paragraph with the appropriate tone from a list of options.

Sample Sentences/Paragraphs:

1. *"The soft rustle of leaves lulled me into a peaceful slumber, a gentle reminder of nature's tranquility."*

2. *"The bustling streets buzzed with energy as crowds hurried past, each lost in their thoughts and ambitions."*

3. *"With a heavy heart, I bid farewell to the familiar streets that had been my home for so long, each step filled with bittersweet memories."*

Tone Options:

A. Reflective
B. Energetic
C. Melancholic
D. Tranquil

Activity 3: Match the Tone

Instructions: Below are four paragraphs written with different tones. Match each paragraph with the tone that best reflects its style and mood. Select the most appropriate tone from the provided options.

Paragraphs:

1. *"The sun dipped below the horizon, casting a golden hue across the sky. As I walked along the beach, the gentle lapping of the waves echoed in my ears, a soothing melody that calmed my racing thoughts."*
2. *"In the heart of the bustling city, skyscrapers towered overhead, their steel frames glinting in the sunlight. Amidst the chaos of the streets, I found solace in the anonymity of the crowd, a silent observer in the urban jungle."*
3. *"The forest enveloped me in its cool embrace, the rustle of leaves like whispers in the wind. Each step I took echoed through the silent trees, a symphony of solitude."*
4. *"With a heavy heart, I bid farewell to the familiar streets that had been my home for so long, each step filled with bittersweet memories."*

Tone Options:

A. Reflective
B. Energetic
C. Melancholic
D. Tranquil

7. Proofreading and Final Touches

This chapter explores the crucial stage of proofreading and adding final touches to our paragraphs. Let's delve into effective strategies tailored to high schoolers, ensuring perfect writing.

Importance of Proofreading in the Editing Process:

Proofreading ensures your writing is error-free and effectively communicates your ideas. For example, imagine you've written a paragraph discussing the benefits of extracurricular activities. Through proofreading, you catch spelling errors like "extracurricular," ensuring your message is clear and professional.

Strategies for Effective Proofreading:

- **Reading Aloud:** Reading your paragraph out loud is an effective way to spot awkward phrasing and grammatical errors in your writing. For instance, reading an essay about your summer vacation and repeatedly noticing the phrase "We had fun" can prompt you to find alternative ways to express enjoyment.

- **Using Proofreading Symbols:** Familiarize yourself with symbols such as "^" to insert text and "sp" to correct spelling errors. For example, while proofreading an essay on environmental conservation, use the "^" symbol to add information about recycling initiatives in your community.

Common Errors to Watch Out for in Paragraphs:

- **Grammar and Spelling Mistakes:** When analyzing the impact of technology on society, it is essential to look for grammatical errors and misspelled words. For instance, in your paragraph, you noticed a misspelling of "technological" as "technolgical."

- **Sentence Structure**: Ensure sentences are clear and properly structured. For example, in your paragraph discussing the benefits of reading, you notice a run-on sentence and break it into two concise sentences for clarity.

Final Checklist for Perfecting Paragraphs:

Before finalizing your paragraphs, use a checklist to cover all elements. This includes checking for grammatical errors, reviewing sentence structure, and confirming that your paragraph stays on topic. For instance, before submitting your essay on time management, you check your final checklist to ensure your paragraphs flow logically and effectively support your main argument.

Activity: Proofreading Practice Passage

Sample Paragraph:

"The excitement of the upcoming school dance was palpable. Students buzzed with anticipation as they chatted animatedly in the hallways, discussing outfits, dates, and dance moves. However, amidst the excitement, there was an air of nervousness as well. For many, this would be their first school dance experience, and the pressure to impress was tangible. Nevertheless, as the music began to play and the lights dimmed, all worries faded away, and the dance floor came alive with laughter and joy."

Editing Example:

After proofreading the paragraph, you notice errors:

- *Spelling mistake: "animatdely" should be "animatedly"*

- *Punctuation error: Replace the comma after "however" with a semicolon*

- *Clarification needed: Rephrase "all worries faded away, and the dance floor came alive" for clarity, such as "all worries vanished as the dance floor lit up with laughter and joy."*

Correcting these errors and making necessary revisions ensures your paragraph is polished and effectively conveys your message. Proofreading and final touches are essential for presenting your ideas clearly and leaving a lasting impact on your readers.

After proofreading, here's the corrected paragraph:

"*The excitement of the upcoming school dance was palpable. Students buzzed with anticipation as they chatted animatedly in the hallways, discussing outfits, dates, and dance moves. However, amidst the excitement, there was an air of nervousness as well. For many, this would be their first school dance experience, and the pressure to impress was tangible. Nevertheless, as the music began to play and the lights dimmed, all worries vanished as the dance floor lit up with laughter and joy.*"

In this revised version, I've corrected the spelling mistake "animatdely" to "animatedly," replaced the comma after "however" with a semicolon for proper punctuation, and rephrased "all worries faded away, and the dance floor came alive" for clarity and coherence.

Trivia Corner

- *The "Fresh Baked Children" bakery mishap: A bakery intended to promote its freshly baked goods but mistakenly displayed a sign that read "Fresh Baked Children" instead. The humorous blunder quickly spread on social media, reminding readers of the importance of proofreading signs and advertisements.*

- *The "Missing Comma" court case: In 2017, a court ruling in Maine turned on the absence of a serial comma in a legal document, costing a company millions of dollars. The case underscored the critical role of proper punctuation and proofreading in legal contracts and documents to avoid costly misunderstandings.*

- *The "Dear Aunt Jane" email failed: A heartfelt email intended for "Dear Aunt Jean" mistakenly addressed the recipient as "Dear Aunt Jane." The sender's embarrassment was compounded when they realized the auto-correct error had changed the recipient's name. This humorous blunder serves as a reminder to always double-check recipients' names before hitting send.*

 ACTIVITY CORNER 7

Activity 1

Instructions: The passage contains deliberate grammar, spelling, and punctuation errors. Ask them to identify and correct these errors.

Sample Passage: *"The studdents wer struggeling with theyr assighnments. They're writing was full of speling errors and improper punctuation. It was hard too follow their idees wen reding."*

Activity 2

Instructions: Below are sentences containing errors . Proofread them.

Sample Sentences:

1. The dog's bark was loud and echo'd through the neighborhood.
2. She likes to walk her dog, cook dinner, and relaxing in the evening.
3. They're going to there friend's house to play there new video game.

Activity 3: Proofreading Checklist Quiz

Instructions:
Below is a list of statements about proofreading; identify whether each statement is true or false.

Sample Statements:

1. Proofreading involves checking for errors in grammar, spelling, and punctuation.
2. Reading your writing aloud can help you identify awkward phrasing and errors.
3. Proofreading is not necessary if you have already spell-checked your document.
4. A final checklist can help ensure that all necessary elements are reviewed before finalizing your writing.

8. Applying Paragraph Editing Skills

1) Integrating Paragraph Editing Skills into Writing Projects:

Mastering paragraph editing skills in high school is vital for creating clear, cohesive, and effective written work. It involves applying various editing techniques to refine paragraphs, ensuring they convey ideas accurately and engage readers. Here's an example paragraph:

Original Paragraph:

"I love spending time outdoors, especially during the summer. There's something about the warm sunshine and gentle breeze that makes me feel alive. Whether it's hiking through the mountains or lounging by the beach, I find solace in nature."

Applying Paragraph Editing Skills:

Topic Sentence: The original paragraph lacks a clear topic sentence. Let's start with a topic sentence that introduces the main idea.

Revised: "Spending time outdoors rejuvenates my spirit and provides a much-needed escape from the hustle and bustle of everyday life."

Supporting Details: While the paragraph describes the author's love for nature, it lacks specific examples or details. Let's add concrete details to enhance clarity and engagement.

Revised: "Whether it's hiking along winding trails, swimming in pristine lakes, or watching fiery sunsets, each outdoor adventure fills me with joy and gratitude."

Concluding Sentence: The original paragraph ends abruptly without summarizing the main points. Let's add a concluding sentence to wrap up the paragraph.

Revised: "In nature's embrace, I find peace, inspiration, and a renewed sense of purpose."

2) Real-world applications of Paragraph Editing in Academic and Professional Settings:

Mastering paragraph editing skills has real-world applications beyond high school in academic and professional settings.

Original Paragraph:

"Effective communication is crucial for success in both academic and professional environments. Whether it's writing research papers or composing business reports, the ability to convey ideas clearly and persuasively is invaluable."

Applying Paragraph Editing Skills:

Relevance to Audience: *While the paragraph mentions the importance of communication, it lacks specificity regarding paragraph editing skills. Let's make the paragraph more relevant by focusing on editing.*

Revised: *"Mastering paragraph editing skills is essential for producing clear, concise, and compelling written communication in academic and professional settings. Whether drafting essays, reports, or presentations, precise editing ensures ideas are conveyed effectively and professionally."*

Supporting Details: *The paragraph briefly mentions academic and professional communication but lacks specific examples of how paragraph editing skills are applied. Let's add concrete examples to illustrate the importance of editing.*

Revised: *"In academia, students must meticulously edit essays and research papers to meet academic standards and convey complex ideas effectively. Similarly, professionals rely on precise editing to craft persuasive proposals, reports, and emails that resonate with their audience."*

Concluding Sentence: *The original paragraph ends abruptly without summarizing the main points. Let's add a concluding sentence to reinforce the importance of paragraph editing skills.*

Revised: *"In today's competitive landscape, mastering paragraph editing skills is a valuable asset that enhances academic performance and professional success."*

3) Tips for Sustaining Good Editing Habits Beyond High School:

Developing and maintaining good editing habits is crucial for long-term writing success. Proofreading for spelling, grammar, and punctuation errors is important. Additionally, taking breaks between writing and editing sessions to review work with fresh eyes is helpful.

Original Paragraph:

"As students progress through high school, they encounter increasingly complex writing assignments that require careful editing and revision. To excel in these tasks, students must develop effective editing habits that extend beyond high school."

Applying Paragraph Editing Skills:

Actionable Advice: *While the paragraph mentions the importance of good editing habits, it lacks specific tips or strategies for sustaining them. Let's provide actionable advice to help students develop effective editing habits.*

Revised: *"To sustain good editing habits beyond high school, students can establish a systematic editing process that includes proofreading for grammar, punctuation, and clarity. Creating a checklist of common errors, seeking feedback from peers or mentors, and revising drafts multiple times are effective strategies for refining writing skills."*

Supporting Details: *The paragraph discusses the importance of editing habits but lacks specific examples or strategies. Add concrete examples to illustrate how students can sustain good editing habits.*

Revised: *"By dedicating dedicated time for editing, utilizing editing tools such as grammar checkers and style guides, and actively seeking feedback from professors or colleagues, students can develop and maintain effective editing habits that enhance the quality of their writing."*

Concluding Sentence: *The original paragraph ends abruptly without summarizing the main points. Let's add a concluding sentence to reinforce the importance of sustaining good editing habits.*

Revised: *"In summary, by incorporating effective editing habits into their writing routine, students can improve their writing skills and achieve academic success both in high school and beyond."*

4) Reflection and Goal Setting for Further Improvement:

Reflecting on writing experiences and setting goals is essential for continuous improvement. For example, it can help you identify areas of weakness and develop strategies to address them.

Original Paragraph:

"As students navigate through various writing assignments in high school, they encounter opportunities for reflection and goal setting. Students can set achievable goals for further improvement by evaluating their strengths and weaknesses."

Applying Paragraph Editing Skills:

Goal Setting and Self-Assessment: *The paragraph mentions reflection and goal setting but lacks specific guidance on implementing these practices. Let's provide strategies for effective goal-setting and self-assessment.*

Revised: *"Students can foster continuous improvement in writing skills by setting specific, measurable, achievable, relevant, and time-bound (SMART) goals. Reflecting on past writing experiences, seeking feedback from teachers or peers, and revising based on feedback are effective strategies for identifying areas of improvement and setting meaningful goals."*

Supporting Details: *The paragraph lacks specific examples or strategies to illustrate how students can implement reflection and goal setting in their writing practice. Let's add concrete examples to make it clearer.*

Revised: *"By setting goals such as improving thesis statement clarity, expanding vocabulary usage, or refining paragraph structure, students can take proactive steps towards enhancing their writing skills. Reflecting on past writing assignments, identifying areas for improvement, and setting specific action plans to address weaknesses are key components of effective goal setting."*

Concluding Sentence: *The original paragraph fails to summarize the main points. A concluding sentence has been added to reinforce the importance of reflection and goal-setting for further improvement.*

Revised: *"In conclusion, by embracing reflection and goal setting as integral parts of the writing process, students can take proactive steps towards enhancing their writing skills and achieving academic success."*

Trivia Corner

- *The famous author Ernest Hemingway once said, "The first draft of anything is garbage." This quote highlights the importance of revising and editing, emphasizing that the initial writing process is just the beginning of crafting polished and impactful writing.*

- *The Power of "There": The overuse of the word "there" as an empty placeholder ("There are many reasons...") can weaken writing. Editing can identify these instances and replace them with stronger sentence structures.*

◎ ACTIVITY CORNER 8

Activity 1 : School Newsletter Editing Project

Objective: To provide practical experience editing real-world documents and enhance proofreading skills.

Sample school newsletter to be edited:

Spring Newsletter

Dear Parents and Students,

We hope this newsletter finds you well! We have some exciting updates and announcements to share with you.

- Please remember that the school carnival is coming up next Saturday. We are still in need of volunteers to help with setup and activities. If you're able to lend a hand, please contact the school office.
- The annual talent show will be held on Friday, May 15th, at 7:00 PM in the school auditorium. Come out and support your fellow classmates as they showcase their talents!
- Don't forget about the upcoming book fair, happening from May 18th to May 22nd. There will be a wide selection of books available for purchase, so be sure to stop by and stock up on your summer reading!

Thank you for your continued support, and we look forward to seeing you at our upcoming events!
Sincerely, The School Newsletter Team

Activity 2 : Proofreading Challenge

Objective: To reinforce proofreading rules, grammar, and punctuation skills through an interactive quiz game.

Sample school newsletter to be edited:

Sample Questions:

1. Which of the following sentences contains a subject-verb agreement error?

a) The dog barks loudly in the park.
b) The cats sleep peacefully on the windowsill.
c) The books was on the shelf.
 d) The students study diligently for their exams.

2. Identify the correct punctuation for the following sentence: "I can't wait to go to the beach it's going to be so much fun."

a) I can't wait to go to the beach. It's going to be so much fun.
b) I can't wait to go to the beach; it's going to be so much fun.
c) I can't wait to go to the beach, it's going to be so much fun.
 d) I can't wait to go to the beach its going to be so much fun.

3. True or False: The "it's" apostrophe indicates possession.

a) True
b) False

4. Which word is misspelled in the following sentence? "She received a surprize gift from her friend."

a) received
 b) surprize
c) gift
d) friend

5. Choose the sentence with the correct use of a semicolon:

 a) I enjoy reading; it helps me relax.
b) I enjoy reading, it helps me relax.
 c) I enjoy reading. It helps me relax.
d) I enjoy reading: it helps me relax.

6. Choose the correct punctuation for the following sentence: "The concert starts at 7:30 p.m"
a) 7:30 p.m,
b) 7:30 p.m;
c) 7:30 p.m.
d) 7:30 p.m?

7. Identify the grammatical error in the following sentence: "Their is two apples left on the table."
a) Their
b) is
c) two
d) on

9. Genre-Specific Editing Techniques

1. Editing Narrative Paragraphs:

- Narrative paragraphs are the backbone of storytelling, weaving characters, settings, and events together to create engaging narratives.

- When editing narrative paragraphs, it's essential to focus on developing characters, advancing the plot, and creating vivid descriptions that immerse readers in the story.

Example Paragraph:

Original: *Sarah walked through the dense forest. It was dark and scary. Suddenly, she heard a noise. She felt scared.*

Edited Paragraph:

Sarah cautiously made her way through the dense forest; her footsteps muffled by the thick blanket of fallen leaves beneath her. Shadows danced around her, casting eerie shapes against the towering trees. A rustling sound caught her attention as she pressed on, sending a shiver down her spine. With her heart pounding in her chest, Sarah's senses heightened, every rustle and creak echoing through the silent woods.

2. Editing Expository Paragraphs:

Expository paragraphs aim to inform and explain, providing readers with clear and organized factual information. When editing expository paragraphs, focus on clarity, organization, and effective presentation of information.

Example Paragraph:

Original: *Volcanoes are formed by hot molten lava erupting from the Earth's surface. They can be dangerous and destructive. Many volcanoes are found along the Ring of Fire.*

Edited Paragraph:

Volcanoes, natural phenomena shaped by the Earth's geological processes, are formed when molten rock, or magma, rises to the surface through vents or fissures. As this magma erupts, it releases gases, ash, and lava, often resulting in explosive or effusive volcanic activity. The Ring of Fire, a horseshoe-shaped zone encircling the Pacific Ocean, is renowned for its high volcanic and seismic activity, hosting numerous active volcanoes that pose risks to nearby communities and ecosystems.

3. Editing Persuasive Paragraphs:

Persuasive paragraphs aim to sway the reader's opinion or persuade them to take a specific action. When editing persuasive paragraphs, it's essential to strengthen arguments, address counterarguments, and appeal to the audience's emotions and logic.

Example Paragraph:

Original: *School uniforms are unnecessary. Students should be allowed to express themselves freely through their clothing choices. Uniforms stifle creativity and individuality.*

Edited Paragraph:

While school uniforms may seem restrictive at first glance, but they serve a vital purpose in promoting student unity and equality. By removing socioeconomic disparities associated with clothing, uniforms create a level playing field where all students are judged based on their merits rather than their attire. Moreover, uniforms instill a sense of pride and belonging within the school community, fostering a conducive learning environment where students can focus on their studies without distractions.

4. Editing Descriptive Paragraphs:

Descriptive paragraphs are a powerful tool to connect the reader and the written piece. They use sensory language and vivid imagery to bring the words to life and paint a clear picture in the mind of the reader. These paragraphs aim to evoke emotions and create vivid mental images as if the reader is experiencing the event or scene described firsthand. When editing descriptive paragraphs, it's crucial to emphasize sensory details, such as sights, sounds, smells, tastes, and textures. Using figurative language, such as metaphors and similes, can also enhance the descriptive nature of the writing. A well-crafted descriptive paragraph can transport the reader to a different world and leave a lasting impression.

Example Paragraph:

Original: *The beach was beautiful. The sand was soft, and the water was blue. There were seashells on the shore.*

Edited Paragraph:

The sun hung low in the sky, casting a golden hue over the tranquil beach. Refined grains of sand, warmed by the afternoon sun, yielded gently underfoot as waves lapped against the shore with rhythmic whispers. The cerulean expanse of the ocean stretched out before me, its surface shimmering like liquid sapphire beneath the midday sun. Along the water's edge, an array of seashells glistened like scattered jewels, each one a testament to the ocean's bounty.

5. Editing Analytical Paragraphs:

Analytical paragraphs explore the deeper meanings and interpretations of texts, ideas, or phenomena. When editing analytical paragraphs, it's crucial to focus on critical thinking, evidence-based analysis, and logical reasoning to support arguments and interpretations.

Example Paragraph:

Original: The protagonist of the novel is brave. She faces many challenges throughout the story and overcomes them all.

Edited Paragraph:

The protagonist is portrayed as a brave and resilient character, a central theme throughout the novel. From her initial struggles to her eventual triumphs, the protagonist demonstrates unwavering courage and determination in the face of adversity. Through her actions and choices, she embodies the essence of bravery, inspiring readers to confront their own challenges with fortitude and resilience.

TRIVIA CORNER

- *During the Civil Rights Movement in the United States, powerful speeches such as Martin Luther King Jr.'s "I Have a Dream" speech showcased the persuasive power of language in advocating for social change.*

- *Investigative reporting has uncovered numerous scandals and corruption in journalism, highlighting the importance of factual accuracy and thorough editing to uphold journalistic integrity.*

- *In literature, iconic authors like William Shakespeare revolutionized storytelling with their use of language and narrative techniques, demonstrating the enduring impact of skilled editing on literary works throughout history.*

◎ ACTIVITY CORNER 9

Activity 1 : Match the Following Paragraphs to the Type of Paragraph

Instructions: Below are paragraphs representing different genres. Match each paragraph to its corresponding type of paragraph **(narrative, expository, persuasive, descriptive, analytical).**

1. *Paragraph: "The sun dipped below the horizon, casting a warm glow over the sleepy town. As dusk settled in, the streets came alive with the chatter of neighbors exchanging stories and laughter. Children played tag in the fading light, their joyful shouts echoing through the evening air."*

2. *Paragraph: "Photosynthesis is a biological process used by plants and other organisms to convert light energy into chemical energy. It plays a crucial role in the Earth's ecosystem by producing oxygen and glucose, essential for sustaining life."*

3. *Paragraph: "School uniforms have been a topic of debate for decades. While proponents argue that uniforms promote equality and reduce distractions, opponents contend that they stifle individuality and self-expression among students."*

4. *Paragraph: "The ancient ruins stood silent and majestic against the backdrop of the setting sun. Moss-covered stones whispered tales of bygone civilizations, their secrets buried beneath layers of history and time."*

5. *Paragraph: "Through the lens of feminist theory, the portrayal of female characters in literature reflects broader societal attitudes towards gender roles and power dynamics. By analyzing these representations, scholars gain insight into the cultural values and biases of different periods."*

⦿ ACTIVITY CORNER 9

Activity 2 : Identify Paragraph Type and Rectify Errors

Instructions: Below are paragraphs representing different types of paragraphs. Identify the type of paragraph for each and then find and rectify any errors present in the paragraph.

1. ***Paragraph***: *"The first step in photosynthesis is light. Plants use sunlight to convert water and carbon dioxide into glucose and oxygen. This process is essential for plant growth and the production of oxygen, which is necessary for all living organisms."*
2. ***Paragraph***: *"The clock struck midnight, and the eerie silence of the night enveloped the old mansion. Shadows danced along the walls, casting strange shapes in the moonlight. Suddenly, a loud crash echoed through the hallway, sending shivers down my spine."*
3. ***Paragraph***: *"Global warming is a pressing issue that affects our planet. It is caused by greenhouse gas emissions, such as carbon dioxide and methane, which trap heat in the Earth's atmosphere. This leads to rising temperatures, melting ice caps, and extreme weather events."*
4. ***Paragraph***: *"School uniforms have been a topic of debate for many years. Some people believe that uniforms promote discipline and unity among students. However, others argue that uniforms restrict individuality and creativity."*
5. ***Paragraph***: *"In Shakespeare's play 'Hamlet,' the protagonist grapples with themes of revenge, madness, and mortality. Through soliloquies and dialogue, Shakespeare explores the complexities of human nature and the consequences of one's actions."*

10. Practicing Paragraph Perfection

Welcome to this chapter, which is dedicated to improving your paragraph writing skills. Like essays, perfecting the craft of crafting paragraphs demands practice, self-evaluation, and positive feedback. Let's delve into some captivating exercises tailored to assist you in becoming a proficient paragraph writer.

Paragraph Prompts for Practice

Here are some stimulating prompts to ignite your imagination and challenge your writing abilities:

- **Character Spotlight:** Choose a character from your favorite book or movie and write a descriptive paragraph that brings them to life. Explore their appearance, personality, and motivations in vivid detail.

- **Setting Exploration**: Transport your readers to a new world by describing a fantastical or exotic setting. Whether it's a bustling metropolis, a serene forest glade, or an alien planet, paint a picture with your words.

- **Dialogue Dynamics**: Craft a dialogue-driven paragraph between two characters discussing a significant event or decision. Focus on capturing the nuances of speech and revealing character relationships through conversation.

- **Emotional Snapshot:** Write a paragraph that captures a moment of intense emotion, such as joy, sadness, fear, or excitement. Use sensory details and expressive language to convey the feelings evoked by the scene.

- **Flash Fiction**: Challenge yourself to tell a complete story in a single paragraph. Pack in all the essential elements of plot, character, and conflict to create a compelling narrative in miniature.

Self-Evaluation and Reflection: Refining Your Craft

Upon completing each practice paragraph, take some time to reflect on your writing and assess your progress. Ask yourself the following questions:

- Did I effectively convey my intended message or evoke the desired emotion in this paragraph?

- Was my writing clear, concise, and engaging?

- Did I use descriptive language and sensory details to bring my paragraph to life?

- Were my sentences varied in length and structure, enhancing the flow and rhythm of the paragraph?

- Did I adhere to grammar and punctuation rules, ensuring my writing is polished and professional?

- What new techniques or strategies did I experiment with in this paragraph, and how did they contribute to its effectiveness?

Peer Review Activities

Collaborating with peers for writing exercises can provide valuable insights and perspectives. Here's how to make the most of this process:

- Swap paragraphs with a writing partner and provide feedback on each other's work, focusing on strengths and areas for improvement.

- Offer suggestions for enhancing clarity, coherence, and impact in your partner's paragraph while acknowledging what they did well.

- Encourage your partner to consider alternative word choices, sentence structures, or organizational strategies that could strengthen their paragraph.

- Remember to approach peer review with empathy and respect, recognizing that constructive criticism is meant to help each other grow as writers.

By engaging in these exercises and reflecting on your writing, you'll continue to refine your paragraph editing skills and become a more confident and influential writer.

⊚ACTIVITY CORNER 10

Activity 1: Paragraph Reconstruction Puzzle

Instructions:

- Provide the reader with a paragraph that has been deliberately scrambled or jumbled.
- Ask them to rearrange the sentences to reconstruct the paragraph in its correct order.
- Once the reader has completed the task, they can check their solution against the provided answer key.

Sample Paragraph (Scrambled):

A. *The sun was setting in a spectacular display of colors.*
B. *Birds chirped happily in the trees, adding to the peaceful ambiance.*
C. *Children laughed and played in the park, their joy infectious.*
D. *Families picnicked on the grass, enjoying quality time together.*
E. *The gentle breeze rustled the leaves, creating a soothing melody*

Activity 2: Spot the Error Challenge

Instructions:

Read the paragraph below and identify any grammar, punctuation, or clarity errors. Once you've spotted the errors, provide the corrected version of the paragraph.

Sample Paragraph :

I went too the store yesterday to buy some grocerees. Their was a long line at the checkout, so I decided too wait. Finally, it was my turn and I handed the cashier my cart. She rang up my items quickly and I payed with my credit card. After leaving the store, I realized I forgot too grab milk, so I went back inside to get it.

ACTIVITY ANSWERS

ACTIVITY CORNER 1

Paragraph 1: Is Social Media Making You Sad?

Corrected Paragraph:

Social media has become an undeniable force, shaping the way we connect and stay informed. However, its impact isn't always positive. Platforms teeming with users can foster negativity and unrealistic expectations. Many users meticulously craft online personas, showcasing only their best moments. This carefully constructed image can lead to feelings of inadequacy and insecurity, particularly among teenagers whose self-esteem is still under development.

Explanation:

- *We removed the unnecessary phrase "millions of users worldwide."*
- *I have replaced "There's a flip side to this coin" with the more specific "However, its impact isn't always positive."*
- *Changed "breeding ground" to the more formal "teeming with users."*
- *Explained "curated version" by using "meticulously craft online personas."*
- *Replaced "highlight reels" with the more formal "carefully constructed image."*
- *Used "insecurity" instead of "envy" for a more nuanced emotional impact.*

Paragraph 2: The Future of Jobs

Corrected Paragraph:

The rise of automation is forcing high schoolers to confront a crucial question: what careers will be available by graduation? This shift can leave them feeling overwhelmed and unsure of which path to take. However, the future of work isn't all negative! New job opportunities are constantly popping up, particularly in fields that require creative problem-solving and adaptability. By honing these essential skills, high schoolers can ensure their success, regardless of the specific job title they hold in the ever-evolving workforce.

Explanation:

- *"Rapidly taking over" - A bit dramatic. Consider "increasingly automating."*
- *"This uncertainty can be stressful." - This is a weak opening.*
- *"Doom and gloom" - Cliche.*
- *"New job opportunities are constantly emerging" - Passive voice.*

ACTIVITY CORNER 2

PARAGRAPH 1: EXPLORING THE COSMOS

Topic Sentence:

"The exploration of space has always fascinated humankind."

Supporting Details:

- "From the first glimpse of the moon through telescopes to the landing of rovers on distant planets, humans have been driven by a desire to understand the universe beyond Earth."
- "With advancements in technology, space exploration has reached new heights, allowing us to probe the depths of our solar system and beyond."
- "Astronauts face numerous risks, from exposure to cosmic radiation to the psychological effects of long-duration space travel."

Concluding Sentence:

"Despite these challenges, the quest for knowledge and discovery continues to fuel our exploration of the final frontier."

Solution Paragraph:

"The exploration of space has always fascinated humankind. From the first glimpse of the moon through telescopes to the landing of rovers on distant planets, humans have been driven to understand the universe beyond Earth. With advancements in technology, space exploration has reached new heights, allowing us to probe the depths of our solar system and beyond. Astronauts face numerous risks, from exposure to cosmic radiation to the psychological effects of long-duration space travel. Despite these challenges, the quest for knowledge and discovery continues to fuel our exploration of the final frontier."

ACTIVITY CORNER 2

PARAGRAPH 2: CONFRONTING CLIMATE CHANGE

Topic Sentence:

"Climate change poses significant challenges to our planet's ecosystems."

Supporting Details:

- "Rising global temperatures are leading to melting ice caps, causing sea levels to rise and threatening coastal communities."
- "Extreme weather events, such as hurricanes and wildfires, are becoming more frequent and severe, wreaking havoc on both human populations and natural habitats."
- "Shifts in precipitation patterns are affecting agriculture and food security, leading to potential famine in some regions."

Concluding Sentence:

"It is imperative that we take urgent action to mitigate the impacts of climate change and protect our planet for future generations."

Reconstructed Paragraph:

"Climate change poses significant challenges to our planet's ecosystems. Rising global temperatures are leading to melting ice caps, causing sea levels to rise and threatening coastal communities. Extreme weather events like hurricanes and wildfires are becoming more frequent and severe, wreaking havoc on human populations and natural habitats. Shifts in precipitation patterns are affecting agriculture and food security, leading to potential famine in some regions. We must take urgent action to mitigate the impacts of climate change and protect our planet for future generations."

ACTIVITY CORNER 3

Paragraph 1:

(1) I love spending time outdoors. (2) Additionally, I often go for long walks in the park. (3) The fresh air and greenery help me relax. (4) My favorite spot is the lake. (5) Surrounded by tall trees, it's a perfect escape. (6) Moreover, there, I can sit and read for hours. (7) As a result, I feel a sense of peace by the water.

Paragraph 2:

(1) I enjoy experimenting in the kitchen. (2) Furthermore, I like trying out new recipes. (3) Cooking allows me to express my creativity. (4) However, sometimes things don't turn out as expected. (5) Despite this, it can be frustrating. (6) Nevertheless, I've learned to laugh off culinary mishaps. (7) Consequently, it's all part of the learning process.

Paragraph 3:

(1) I woke up early in the morning. (2) Subsequently, I hurriedly got dressed. (3) As a result, I had an important meeting to attend. (4) Consequently, I left the house without having breakfast. (5) Luckily, I caught the bus just in time. (6) Consequently, I arrived at the office feeling anxious.

Paragraph 4:

(1) My cat is a mischievous little creature. (2) Consequently, she often gets into trouble. (3) Last night, she knocked over a vase yesterday. (4) Oblivious to the mess, she didn't seem to realize what she'd done. (5) Nevertheless, she continued to play as if nothing had happened. (6) Therefore, she's always keeping me on my toes.

ACTIVITY CORNER 4

Solution Pagaraph 1

"I went for a walk in the park on a lovely day. The sun was shining brightly in the sky, and the birds were singing happily in the trees. As I strolled, I noticed the flowers blooming beautifully in the garden."

Solution Paragraph 2

"My friend lives in a big, yellow house with a garden full of flowers. We often visit to play and have fun."

Solution Paragraph 3

"Early in the morning, I woke up and brushed my teeth before enjoying breakfast. Then, I walked to school where I met my friends and attended classes. After returning home, I completed my homework before heading to bed."

ACTIVITY CORNER 5

Solution: Unity and Coherence Quiz:

Paragraph 1 (Revised): *"I woke up early in the morning and had breakfast with my family. Afterward, I enjoyed a refreshing walk in the park, where I listened to the birds chirping in the trees under the bright morning sun."*

Explanation: The sentences in the original paragraph were disjointed, lacking a clear focus or progression. To improve coherence, I combined the activities into a single morning routine, starting with waking up and having breakfast, followed by a walk in the park. This creates a smoother flow of ideas and maintains a consistent theme throughout the paragraph.

Paragraph 2 *(Unchanged): "My favorite hobbies are reading, playing basketball, and painting. Reading allows me to relax and escape into different worlds. Playing basketball helps me stay active and socialize with friends. Painting allows me to express my creativity and emotions."*

Explanation: This paragraph demonstrates coherence by discussing three hobbies and their respective benefits. Each sentence relates to the central theme of hobbies and provides supporting details effectively. No revision is needed.

ACTIVITY CORNER 5

Paragraph 3 (Revised):

"One destination at the top of my travel bucket list is Paris, where I dream of seeing the iconic Eiffel Tower. Exploring famous landmarks like the Great Wall of China and relaxing on the beautiful beaches of Hawaii are also high on my list. Traveling allows me to immerse myself in new cultures and broaden my horizons."

Explanation: The original paragraph's list of places to visit lacked unity as there was no apparent connection between them. To improve unity, I focused on one specific destination, Paris, and expanded upon the reasons for wanting to visit. I then briefly mentioned other desired destinations while emphasizing the theme of travel and cultural exploration. This creates a more cohesive and unified paragraph with a central focus.

Paragraph Puzzle Challenge:

Revised Paragraph: "As we arrived at the beach, we spread our beach towels and set up an umbrella for shade. Children immediately began building sandcastles while adults relaxed and soaked up the sun. The waves crashed against the shore, creating a soothing sound as seagulls soared overhead, searching for food scraps. After swimming and playing games, we enjoyed a picnic lunch on the sand, savoring the sights and sounds of a perfect day at the beach."

Matching Activity: Matching Paragraph Types

Solution:

- **Paragraph 1: B. Narrative**: This paragraph chronologically recounts events and describes the narrator's morning routine.

- **Paragraph 2: A. Expository:** This paragraph presents facts and explanations about the writer's hobbies and their respective benefits.

- **Paragraph 3: C. Descriptive:** This paragraph vividly describes the writer's travel aspirations and experiences, focusing on sensory details and imagery.

ACTIVITY CORNER 6

ACTIVITY 1: STYLE AND TONE ANALYSIS

Answer:

1. A. Reflective
2. B. Detached
3. C. Introspective

ACTIVITY 2 : TONE MATCHING GAME

Answer:

1. D. Tranquil
2. B. Energetic
3. C. Melancholic

ACTIVITY 3 : TONE MATCHING GAME

Answer:

1. D. Tranquil
2. B. Energetic
3. A. Reflective
4. C. Melancholic

ACTIVITY CORNER 7

ACTIVITY 1: PROOFREADING PRACTICE PASSAGE

Answer: *"The students were struggling with their assignments. Their writing was full of spelling errors and improper punctuation. It was hard to follow their ideas when reading."*

ACTIVITY 2 : PROOFREADING PRACTICE SENTENCES

1. The dog's bark was loud and echo'd through the neighborhood.
Correction: *The dog's bark was loud and echoed through the neighborhood.*
Changes made: *Replaced "echo'd" with "echoed" to correct the spelling.*

2. She likes to walk her dog, cook dinner, and relaxing in the evening.
Correction: *She likes to walk her dog, cook dinner, and relax in the evening.*
Changes made: *Replaced "relaxing" with "relax" to correct the verb form.*

3. They're going to there friend's house to play there new video game.
Correction: *They're going to their friend's house to play their new video game.*
Changes made: *Replaced "there" with "their" for possessive, and "there" with "their" for possessive again.*

ACTIVITY 3 : PROOFREADING CHECKLIST QUIZ

Answers:
   1. True
   2. True
   3. False
   4. True

ACTIVITY CORNER 8

ACTIVITY 1: SCHOOL NEWSLETTER EDITING PROJECT

Revised Version:

Spring Newsletter

Dear Parents and Students,

We hope this newsletter finds you well! We have some exciting updates and announcements to share with you.

- Please remember that the school carnival is coming up next Saturday. We still need volunteers to help with setup and activities. If you can lend a hand, please contact the school office.
- The annual talent show will be held on Friday, May 15th, at 7:00 PM in the school auditorium. Come out and support your fellow classmates as they showcase their talents!
- Don't forget about the upcoming book fair from May 18th to May 22nd. A wide selection of books will be available for purchase, so be sure to stop by and stock up on your summer reading!

Thank you for your continued support, and we look forward to seeing you at our upcoming events!

Sincerely, The School Newsletter Team

List of Corrections
- *Corrected punctuation errors (e.g., missing commas, apostrophes).*
- *Fixed spelling mistakes (e.g., "May" instead of "My").*
- *Ensured consistency in formatting and style (e.g., capitalization, spacing).*
- *Improved clarity and conciseness of sentences (e.g., removed redundant phrases).*
- *Checked for grammatical errors and made necessary revisions.*

ACTIVITY CORNER 8

ACTIVITY 2: PROOFREADING CHALLENGE

Proofreading Quiz Solutions:

1. Which of the following sentences is correctly punctuated?
- Solution: "I can't wait to see you tonight" is correctly punctuated with an apostrophe in "can't" to indicate a contraction.

2. Identify the grammatical error in the following sentence: "Their going to the beach tomorrow."
- Solution: The correct answer is "Their going to the beach tomorrow." The error is the incorrect use of "their" instead of "they're," which is a contraction for "they are."

3. Choose the correctly spelled word:
- Solution: The correct spelling is "necessary."

4. Which sentence is grammatically incorrect?
- Solution: The grammatically incorrect sentence is: "He don't have time to finish his homework." The correct form should be "He doesn't have time to finish his homework."

5. Identify the error in the following sentence: "The dog buried it's bone in the backyard."
- Solution: The error is in the use of "it's," which is a contraction for "it is" or "it has." In this case, it should be "its" without an apostrophe to indicate possession.

6. Choose the correct punctuation for the following sentence: "The concert starts at 7:30 p.m"
- Solution: The correct punctuation is option c) 7:30 p.m.

7. Identify the grammatical error in the following sentence: "Their is two apples left on the table."
- Solution: The grammatical error is option a) Their. The corrected sentence should be: "There are two apples left on the table."

ACTIVITY CORNER 9

ACTIVITY 1 : MATCH THE FOLLOWING PARAGRAPHS TO THE TYPE OF PARAGRAPH

Solution:

1. Descriptive Paragraph
2. Expository Paragraph
3. Persuasive Paragraph
4. Narrative Paragraph
5. Analytical Paragraph

ACTIVITY 1 : IDENTIFY PARAGRAPH TYPE AND RECTIFY ERRORS

Solution:

1. Expository Paragraph - Error: Missing period after "light." Correction: "The first step in photosynthesis is light. Plants use sunlight..."
2. Narrative Paragraph - Error: Comma splice after "midnight." Correction: "The clock struck midnight. The eerie silence of the night..."
3. Expository Paragraph - No errors.
4. Persuasive Paragraph - No errors.
5. Analytical Paragraph - No errors.

ACTIVITY CORNER 10

ACTIVITY 1: PARAGRAPH RECONSTRUCTION PUZZLE

Solution:

The correct order of the paragraph is: C - D - E - B - A.

ACTIVITY 2 : SPOT THE ERROR CHALLENGE

Solution:

I went to the store yesterday to buy some groceries. There was a long line at the checkout, so I decided to wait. Finally, it was my turn, and I handed the cashier my cart. She rang up my items quickly, and I paid with my credit card. After leaving the store, I realized I forgot to grab milk, so I went back inside to get it.

Explanation:

1. *"too" should be "to" in both instances (e.g., "to the store" and "to wait").*
2. *"Their" should be "There" (e.g., "There was a long line").*
3. *"payed" should be "paid" (past tense of "pay").*
4. *"too" should be "to" (e.g., "forgot to grab").*
5. *The paragraph lacks a comma after "Finally" to separate introductory adverbial phrases.*

11. Ten Sample & Ten Practice Paragraphs

EDITING EXERCISE 1

THE POWER OF MUSIC AND MEMORIES

Original Paragraph:
(*Theme: Power of Music, Topic: Emotional Connection, Tone: Informative, Type of Paragraph: Introductory*)

Music is like magic. It can make you happy, sad, or angry. It can take you back to a special time in your life or make you want to dance all night. Music is all around us, in movies, tv shows, and even the grocery store. It's a powerful tool that can change your mood instantly.

Hints to make changes: This paragraph remains focused on the theme (Power of Music) and serves its purpose as an introductory paragraph. However, we can improve it by incorporating the following:

Sensory Details: While the paragraph discusses emotions, adding specific sensory details related to music would create a more evocative experience.

Word Choice: "Magic" and "tool" are generic terms. Consider using stronger verbs and adjectives to convey the power of music.

Revised Paragraph :

THE POWER OF MUSIC AND MEMORIES

<u>Solution</u>

This paragraph remains focused on the theme (Power of Music) and serves its purpose as an introductory paragraph. However, we can improve it by incorporating the following:

- **Sensory Details:** While the paragraph discusses emotions, adding specific sensory details related to music would create a more evocative experience. (For example, instead of "sad," describe the melancholic melody or the bittersweet lyrics.)

- **Word Choice:** "Magic" and "tool" are generic terms. Consider using stronger verbs and adjectives to convey the power of music. (e.g., "Music can orchestrate" or "possesses an undeniable power.")

<u>Revised Paragraph</u>

The first notes of a familiar song can orchestrate a powerful emotional journey. A melancholic melody might evoke a bittersweet pang of nostalgia, while a driving rhythm can ignite an urge to tap your feet or move your body with uninhibited joy. Music isn't just background noise; it possesses an undeniable power to transport us back to cherished memories. The opening chords of a favorite childhood song can paint a vivid picture of a summer road trip, while the pulsing bass line of a recently discovered track might make you yearn to lose yourself on a crowded dance floor. Music weaves itself into the fabric of our experiences, becoming a powerful soundtrack to our lives.

PRACTICE PARAGRAPH 1

Prompt:

Theme: Power of Sensory Details in Writing
Topic: Describing a favorite food (use the revised structure and incorporate specific sensory details)
Tone: Descriptive
Type of Paragraph: Introductory paragraph

Write an introductory paragraph about your favorite food, focusing on using vivid sensory details to create a mouthwatering description.

EDITING EXERCISE 2

THE ALLURE OF SCI-FI NOVELS

Original Paragraph:
(*Theme: Entertainment - Reading, Topic: Science Fiction Novels, Tone: Informative, Type of Paragraph: Introductory - Needs Editing*)

Books are fun to read. They can be exciting and adventurous, and they let you travel to different worlds and experience new things. You can read by yourself or with someone else, and there's a book out there for everyone. Reading is a great way to spend your free time.

Hints to make changes: This paragraph is like a book jacket summarizing the plot generically. Instead of just saying science fiction novels are exciting and adventurous, use specific details to make the reader imagine themself on a thrilling journey through space or encountering fascinating alien civilizations.

Revised Paragraph :

THE ALLURE OF SCI-FI NOVELS

<u>Solution</u>

This paragraph is quite basic and lacks depth. Here's how we can improve it:

- **Show, Don't Tell:** Instead of simply saying "exciting" and "adventurous," use descriptive language to showcase these aspects. (e.g., Describe the feeling of awe as you hurtle through a wormhole or the adrenaline rush of a spaceship chase.)

- **Target Audience:** Consider the age group of the reader. Mention popular tropes or concepts in science fiction that would be relatable to them. (e.g., Mention encountering intelligent robots, exploring distant planets, or battling for survival against a hostile alien invasion.)

<u>Revised Paragraph</u>

Buckle up and prepare for warp speed! Science fiction novels propel us on exhilarating journeys through the vast cosmos. Imagine hurtling through a swirling wormhole, the fabric of space-time distorting around your spacecraft or facing off against a fleet of menacing alien warships, the lasers blazing a deadly ballet across the inky blackness. Science fiction isn't just about futuristic technology; it's about exploring profound questions about humanity, our place in the universe, and the potential wonders (or dangers) that await us amongst the stars. Whether you crave the thrill of interstellar exploration, the philosophical musings on artificial intelligence, or the heart-pounding action of an alien invasion, a science fiction novel is waiting to ignite your imagination.

PRACTICE PARAGRAPH 2

<u>Prompt:</u>

Theme: Entertainment (similar to Reading)
Topic: Food Documentaries (informative or persuasive, your choice)
Tone: Informative
Type of Paragraph: Introductory paragraph

Write your own introductory paragraph about the surprising world of food documentaries, incorporating the revised structure and focusing on specific details that create a mouthwatering picture of the experience.

EDITING EXERCISE 3

THE COMFORT OF COOKING

Original Paragraph:
(Theme: Life Skill - Cooking, Topic: Benefits of Cooking, Tone: Informative, Type of Paragraph: Introductory - Needs Editing)

Cooking can be fun and rewarding. It allows you to be creative and try new things. You can cook for yourself, your family, or friends. There are many different recipes to choose from, so there's something for everyone. Cooking is a great way to relax and unwind after a long day.

Hints to make changes: This paragraph reads like a grocery list of reasons to cook. Instead of just listing benefits, use descriptive language to show how cooking can be a relaxing and creative experience

Revised Paragraph :

THE COMFORT OF COOKING

<u>Solution</u>

This paragraph lacks depth and vivid details. Here's how we can improve it:

- **Sensory Details**: Cooking is a multi-sensory experience. Describe the sights, sounds, and smells that make cooking enjoyable. (e.g., The rhythmic sizzle of ingredients hitting a hot pan, the vibrant colors of fresh vegetables, the warm aroma of spices filling the kitchen.)

- **Emotional Connection:** Highlight the emotional benefits of cooking, such as the satisfaction of creating a delicious meal or the joy of sharing food with loved ones. (e.g., The therapeutic process of chopping vegetables can be a great way to de-stress, while the sense of accomplishment from preparing a tasty meal is truly rewarding.)

 <u>Revised Paragraph</u>

The kitchen isn't just a place to prepare food; it's a haven for creativity and comfort. Imagine the rhythmic sizzle of garlic hitting a hot pan, the vibrant colors of fresh vegetables dancing on the chopping board, and the warm aroma of spices filling the air as they release their essence. Cooking can be a form of therapy, the repetitive motions calming a busy mind, while the satisfaction of creating a delicious meal from scratch is a reward like no other. Sharing the fruits of your labor with loved ones, the laughter and conversation around the dinner table adds another layer of joy to the experience. Cooking nourishes not just the body but also the soul.

PRACTICE PARAGRAPH 3

<u>Prompt:</u>

Theme: Learning (similar to Cooking)
Topic: Taking an Online Course (any subject you choose),
Tone: Persuasive
Type of Paragraph: Introductory paragraph

Write your own introductory paragraph about the unexpected benefits of taking an online course, incorporating the revised structure and focusing on specific details that showcase the convenience and flexibility of online learning.

EDITING EXERCISE 4

THE IMPORTANCE OF RECYCLING

Original Paragraph:
Theme: Environmental Conservation Topic: The Importance of Recycling Tone: Informative Type of Paragraph: Expository

In today's world, where environmental issues are becoming increasingly pressing, recycling plays a vital role in preserving our planet. Recycling helps to conserve natural resources, reduce pollution, and minimize the amount of waste sent to landfills. By sorting and separating recyclable materials such as paper, plastic, glass, and metal, individuals can contribute to the sustainability of our environment. Furthermore, recycling programs in communities and businesses promote awareness and encourage responsible waste management practices.

Hints to make changes: Look for redundancies and unnecessary words to streamline the paragraph for clarity and conciseness.

<u>**Revised Paragraph :**</u>

THE IMPORTANCE OF RECYCLING

<u>Solution</u>

Here's how we can improve it:

- **Remove redundant phrases.**
- **Make sentences more direct and concise.**

<u>Revised Paragraph</u>

In today's world, where environmental issues are increasingly pressing, recycling plays a vital role in preserving our planet. By sorting and separating recyclable materials such as paper, plastic, glass, and metal, individuals contribute to the sustainability of our environment. Recycling helps conserve natural resources, reduces pollution, and minimizes waste sent to landfills. Community and business recycling programs promote awareness and encourage responsible waste management practices.

PRACTICE PARAGRAPH 4

<u>Practice Prompt</u>

Theme: *Environmental Conservation Topic:* **Promoting Sustainable Living** *Tone: Persuasive Type of Paragraph: Argumentative*

Prompt: Write a persuasive paragraph advocating for adopting sustainable living practices in daily life. Discuss the benefits of reducing energy consumption, minimizing waste generation, and supporting eco-friendly initiatives. Encourage readers to take action towards a more sustainable future.

EDITING EXERCISE 5

WHY STUDY ASTRONOMY

Original Paragraph:
Theme: Science - Astronomy, Topic: Why Study Astronomy?, Tone: Informative, Type of Paragraph: Introductory - Needs Editing

Space is cool. It's vast and mysterious, filled with stars, planets, and other things we don't even understand. Studying astronomy can teach you about all of this. You can learn about the history of space exploration, the formation of stars and planets, and even the possibility of life on other worlds. Astronomy is a fascinating subject that can spark your curiosity about the universe.

Hints to make changes: This paragraph reads like a textbook blurb. Instead of just listing facts, use descriptive language to show the awe-inspiring nature of space and the excitement of astronomical discoveries.

Revised Paragraph :

WHY STUDY ASTRONOMY

This paragraph is factual but lacks engagement. Here's how we can improve it:

- **Figurative Language:** Use similes, metaphors, or other figures of speech to paint a vivid picture of the cosmos. (e.g., Imagine a universe teeming with billions of galaxies, each containing countless stars like scattered diamonds on black velvet.)
- **Sense of Wonder**: Highlight the sense of wonder and mystery that astronomy evokes. (e.g., Gazing up at the Milky Way on a clear night, one can't help but ponder the vastness of space and its countless secrets.)

Revised Paragraph:

Astronomy, the study of celestial objects and phenomena, isn't just about memorizing facts and figures. It's a gateway to a universe brimming with awe-inspiring beauty and captivating mysteries. Imagine a universe teeming with billions of galaxies, each containing countless stars like scattered diamonds on black velvet. Peer through a telescope and witness the swirling dance of a nebula, a vast cloud of gas and dust, the birthplace of future stars. Astronomy compels us to ask profound questions about the origins of our universe, the possibility of life on other worlds, and our place in the vast cosmic dance. Whether you're a seasoned stargazer or a curious beginner, the allure of astronomy beckons, inviting you to embark on a lifelong journey of discovery.

PRACTICE PARAGRAPH 5

Practice Prompt

Theme: Learning (similar to Science - Astronomy) Topic**: Learning a New Language** (any language you choose, e.g., Spanish, French, Japanese), Tone: Persuasive Type of Paragraph: Introductory paragraph

Prompt: Write a persuasive paragraph advocating sustainable living practices in daily life. Discuss the benefits of reducing energy consumption, minimizing waste generation, and supporting eco-friendly initiatives. Encourage readers to take action towards a more sustainable future.

EDITING EXERCISE 6

THE THRILL OF DEBATE

Original Paragraph:

Theme: Learning - Communication, Topic: Benefits of Debate, Tone: Informative, Type of Paragraph: Introductory - Needs Editing

Debate is fun. It allows you to learn about different topics and express your opinions. You can debate with friends or classmates; many different debate formats exist. Debate is a great way to improve your communication and critical thinking skills.

Hints to make changes: This paragraph reads like a list of reasons to join the debate team. Instead of just listing benefits, use descriptive language to showcase the excitement and challenge of a good debate.

Revised Paragraph :

THE THRILL OF DEBATE

Solution and Explanation:

This paragraph is basic and lacks the energy of a good debate. Here's how we can improve it:

- Action Verbs: Use strong verbs to capture the dynamic nature of debate. (e.g., "Clash," "parry," "counter-argue")
- Figurative Language: Similes or metaphors can highlight the intellectual sparring aspect of debate. (e.g., "A verbal jousting match")

Revised Paragraph

Imagine the intellectual battlefield: two minds clashing over a controversial topic, each side wielding well-researched arguments like sharpened swords. Debate isn't just about expressing opinions; it's a thrilling exercise in critical thinking and persuasive communication. As you parry your opponent's arguments and counter-argue with logic and evidence, you refine your ability to think on your feet and articulate your ideas with clarity and precision. Debate isn't just for aspiring politicians; it's a valuable skill for anyone who wants to navigate the complexities of the world around them confidently. So, the next time you have a heated discussion with a friend, don't shy away from the challenge – embrace the opportunity to hone your debating skills and emerge with a deeper understanding of the issue.

PRACTICE PARAGRAPH 6

Practice Prompt

Theme: Social (similar to Communication) Topic: **Volunteering** (any cause you choose, e.g., Animal Shelter, Environmental Cleanup), Tone: Persuasive Type of Paragraph: Introductory paragraph

Prompt: Write your own introductory paragraph about the rewarding experience of volunteering, incorporating the revised structure and focusing on specific details that showcase the positive impact you can make on your community.

EDITING EXERCISE 7

THE SATISFACTIONS OF BAKING

Original Paragraph:
Theme: Life Skill - Cooking, Topic: Enjoying Baking, Tone: Informative, Type of Paragraph: Introductory - Needs Editing

Baking is fun. You can be creative and try new recipes. There's something for everyone, from simple cookies to elaborate cakes. Baking is a great way to relax and unwind after a long day. You can also share your creations with friends and family.

Hints to make changes: This paragraph reads like a grocery list of reasons to bake. Instead of just listing benefits, use descriptive language to show the sensory experience and emotional connection of baking.

Revised Paragraph :

THE SATISFACTIONS OF BAKING

Solution and Explanation:

This paragraph lacks details that evoke the senses and emotions. Here's how we can improve it:

- **Sensory Details:** Describe the sights, sounds, and smells that make baking enjoyable. (e.g., the electric mixer's rhythmic creak, vanilla and cinnamon's warm aroma wafting through the kitchen.)

- **Emotional Connection:** Highlight the emotional rewards of baking, such as the satisfaction of creating something delicious or the joy of sharing with loved ones. (For example, kneading dough can be a great way to de-stress, while witnessing your loved ones' smiles as they savor your creation is a truly heartwarming experience.)

Revised Paragraph:

(Type of Paragraph: Body Paragraph - Supporting Point)

The rhythmic creak of the electric mixer becomes a soothing soundtrack as you transform simple ingredients into a culinary masterpiece. The warm aroma of vanilla and cinnamon fills the kitchen, a fragrant promise of deliciousness to come. Baking isn't just about following a recipe; it's a sensory experience that awakens the soul. The therapeutic process of kneading dough allows you to knead away the day's stresses, while the intricate act of decorating a cake becomes a canvas for your creativity.

PRACTICE PARAGRAPH 7

Practice Prompt

Theme: Life Skill (similar to Cooking) Topic: Learning Basic Car Maintenance (oil change, tire change), Tone: Informative Type of Paragraph: Body Paragraph - Step-by-Step Instruction

Prompt: Write your own body paragraph about the steps involved in changing a flat tire, incorporating clear and concise instructions.

EDITING EXERCISE 8

THE ALLURE OF VIDEO GAMES

Original Paragraph:

Theme: Entertainment - Video Games, Topic: Appeal of Video Games, Tone: Informative, Type of Paragraph: Introductory - Needs Editing

Video games are fun. They can be challenging and exciting, and they let you explore different worlds and stories. You can play with friends or alone, and there's a game for everyone. Video games are a great way to pass the time.

Hints to make changes: This paragraph lacks specific details and vivid language. Make it more engaging by showing, not telling.

Revised Paragraph :

THE ALLURE OF VIDEO GAMES

Solution and Explanation:
This paragraph is quite basic and lacks depth. Here's how we can improve it:

- Show, Don't Tell: Instead of simply saying "fun," "challenging," and "exciting," use descriptive language to showcase these aspects. (For example, instead of "challenging," describe the thrill of overcoming a difficult boss fight.)

- Target Audience: Consider the reader's age group. While "exploring different worlds" is a good concept, using more specific and relatable references could be even better (e.g., Mentioning popular game genres like fantasy RPGs or open-world adventures).

Revised Paragraph:

(Type of Paragraph: Conclusion - Restatement & Call to Action)

The captivating world of video games beckons with a unique blend of challenge and excitement. Imagine wielding a powerful sword as you battle mythical creatures in a sprawling fantasy realm, the clash of steel ringing in your ears and the roar of the dragon shaking the ground beneath you. Or perhaps you strategize your way to victory in a fast-paced online competition, your heart pounding as you outmaneuver your opponents and secure the winning shot. Video games allow us to step into the shoes of extraordinary heroes, embark on thrilling adventures, and explore vast, intricately designed worlds—all from the comfort of our homes. Whether you crave the camaraderie of co-op play with friends or the focused intensity of a solo challenge, a video game experience is waiting to be discovered. So, grab your controller, dive in, and prepare to be transported to a world of limitless possibilities.

PRACTICE PARAGRAPH 8

Practice Prompt
Theme: Entertainment (similar to Video Games) **Topic:** Board Games (any specific game or general concept), Tone: Persuasive **Type of Paragraph:** Body Paragraph - Comparison & Contrast

Prompt: Write your own body paragraph about the unique advantages of board games compared to video games, incorporating specific details that highlight the social interaction and strategic thinking aspects.

EDITING EXERCISE 9

THE POWER OF MUSIC

Original Paragraph:
Theme: Art - Music, Topic: Impact of Music on Emotions, Tone: Informative, Type of Paragraph: Introductory - Needs Editing

Music is cool. It can make you feel happy, sad, or relaxed. There are many different genres of music to choose from, so there's something for everyone. Listening to music is a great way to unwind after a long day.

Hints to make changes: This paragraph reads like a simple statement. Use descriptive language and figurative speech to show people's emotional connection with music.

Revised Paragraph :

THE POWER OF MUSIC

Solution and Explanation:
This paragraph lacks depth and vivid details. Here's how we can improve it:

- **Figurative Language:** Use similes, metaphors, or other figures of speech to describe how music affects emotions. (For example, Upbeat music can be a shot of energy, while a melancholic melody can feel like a warm embrace on a rainy day.)

- **Sensory Details:** Consider describing the way music can affect us physically. (For example, the rhythm of a song can get your heart racing, while a soothing melody can calm your nerves.)

Revised Paragraph:

(Type of Paragraph: Body Paragraph - Cause & Effect)

Music isn't just a collection of sounds; it's a powerful language that speaks directly to our emotions. An upbeat melody can be a potent energy shot, its infectious rhythm coaxing your feet to tap and your heart to race. On the other hand, a melancholic ballad can feel like a warm embrace on a rainy day, the poignant lyrics mirroring the ache in your soul. Music has the uncanny ability to mirror our emotions, offering solace in times of sadness and amplifying our joy during moments of celebration. It's a soundtrack to our lives, weaving a tapestry of emotions that resonates deep within us.

PRACTICE PARAGRAPH 9

Practice Prompt
Theme: Art (similar to Music) **Topic:** Photography (any specific type of photography or general concept)**, Tone:** Informative Type of Paragraph: **Body Paragraph -** Definition & Examples

Prompt: Write your own body paragraph about the unique advantages of board games over video games, incorporating specific details that highlight social interaction and strategic thinking.

EDITING EXERCISE 10

THE VALUE OF VOLUNTEERING

Original Paragraph:
Theme: Social Responsibility - Volunteering, Topic: Importance of Volunteering, Tone: Informative, Type of Paragraph: Introductory - Needs Editing

Volunteering is a good thing to do. It helps others and makes you feel good. Many different volunteer opportunities are available, so you can find something that interests you. Volunteering is a great way to give back to your community and make a difference.

Hints to make changes: This paragraph reads like a list of benefits. Instead of just stating facts, use emotional language and specific details to showcase volunteers' impact.

Revised Paragraph :

THE VALUE OF VOLUNTEERING

<u>Solution and Explanation:</u>

This paragraph lacks emotional connection and specifics. Here's how we can improve it:

- **Emotional Language:** Highlight the fulfillment and purpose of volunteering (e.g., the joy of seeing a child's face light up as you read them a story or the satisfaction of knowing you're helping to build a brighter future for your community).
- **Specific Examples:** Provide concrete examples of how volunteering can make a difference. (e.g., Volunteering at a homeless shelter provides essential support to those in need, while cleaning up a local park can create a more enjoyable space for everyone.)

Revised Paragraph:

(Type of Paragraph: Body Paragraph - Cause & Effect)

Imagine a world where a helping hand is readily available to those in need. Volunteering isn't just about checking a box on a college application; it's about making a tangible difference in the lives of others and the world around you. Whether it's spending time with lonely seniors at a nursing home or working tirelessly to clean up a polluted beach, volunteering tackles real-world issues and fosters a sense of community spirit. The joy of seeing a child's face light up as you mentor them or the satisfaction of knowing you've helped build a safer environment in your neighborhood – these are the rewards that come from dedicating your time and talents to a cause you believe in. Volunteering isn't just about giving back; it's about enriching your own life while making a positive impact on the world.

PRACTICE PARAGRAPH 9

<u>Practice Prompt</u>
Theme: Social Responsibility (similar to Volunteering) **Topic:** Recycling (any specific material or general concept)**, Tone:** Persuasive Type of Paragraph: Body Paragraph - Cause & Effect

Prompt: Write your own body paragraph about the unique advantages of board games over video games, incorporating specific details that highlight social interaction and strategic thinking.

12. Prompt Challenge

PROMPT CHALLENGE: EXPLORING PARAGRAPH TOPICS

This chapter will delve into various prompts to challenge your paragraph writing skills. Each activity offers a unique opportunity to explore different topics, hone your writing abilities, and express your thoughts effectively within a structured framework.

Reflective Moment Paragraph:

Prompt: Reflect on a significant moment and write a paragraph exploring its impact on your growth.

Exercise: Think about a moment that had a profound impact on you, such as winning a competition, overcoming a fear, or experiencing a loss. Write a paragraph reflecting on how this moment shaped your character and influenced your perspective on life.

Debating Perspectives Paragraph:

Prompt: Choose a current social issue and write a paragraph presenting two perspectives. Explore the arguments for each viewpoint.

Exercise: Select a controversial topic like climate change, gun control, or social media censorship. Write a paragraph presenting one perspective advocating for action and another expressing skepticism. Support each viewpoint with compelling arguments and evidence.

Book Review Paragraph:

Prompt: Read a book you recently enjoyed. Write a paragraph book review discussing the plot, characters, and your overall recommendation.

Exercise: Read a book of your choice and write a paragraph reviewing it. Summarize the plot briefly, analyze the characters' development, and share your thoughts on the book's strengths and weaknesses. Conclude with a recommendation for potential readers.

Personal Passion Paragraph:

Prompt: Identify a hobby or passion of yours. Using personal anecdotes and examples, write a paragraph exploring why this activity is meaningful to you.

Exercise: Think about a hobby or activity you're passionate about, such as playing an instrument, painting, or volunteering. Write a paragraph explaining why this activity brings you joy, how it has impacted your life, and what lessons you've learned from pursuing it.

Future Aspirations Paragraph:

Prompt: Imagine your life ten years from now. Write a paragraph outlining your future aspirations, career goals, and the steps you plan to take to achieve them.

Exercise: Visualize where you see yourself in ten years. Write a paragraph describing your ideal future, including your career aspirations, personal goals, and the steps you plan to take to turn your dreams into reality. Be specific and realistic in your plans.

Analyzing a Quote Paragraph:

Prompt: Choose a meaningful quote and write a paragraph analyzing its significance. Explore how the quote relates to your life or broader societal themes.

Exercise: Select a quote that resonates with you, such as "The only way to do great work is to love what you do" by Steve Jobs. Write a paragraph dissecting the quote's meaning, discussing its relevance to your life experiences or broader societal implications.

Historical Event Exploration Paragraph:

Prompt: Select a historical event that interests you. Write a paragraph discussing the event's causes, effects, and long-term impacts on society.

Exercise: Choose a historical event, such as the Civil Rights Movement, the Industrial Revolution, or the Fall of the Berlin Wall. Write a paragraph analyzing the event's causes, detailing its effects on society at the time, and discussing its lasting impact on today's world.

Technology's Impact Paragraph:

Prompt: Explore the impact of technology on modern life. Using specific examples, write a paragraph discussing technology's positive and negative effects.

Exercise: Reflect on the role of technology in your daily life and society as a whole. Write a paragraph outlining its positive contributions, such as increased connectivity and efficiency, as well as its negative effects, such as privacy concerns and social isolation.

We'd Love Your Feedback!

Please let us know how we're doing by leaving us a review.

CONCLUSION

Dear aspiring writers, congratulations on completing the Paragraph Editing for the High School workbook! Throughout this journey, you've honed your skills in crafting clear, concise, and engaging paragraphs. You've taken significant strides toward becoming a proficient writer by refining your editing techniques and attention to detail.

But remember, the art of writing is a continuous process of learning and growth. As you embark on your writing endeavors beyond this workbook, carry the tools and insights gained here. Embrace the challenge of refining your paragraphs, always striving for clarity and impact.

Just as every well-edited paragraph enhances the strength of your writing, each revision and refinement you make contributes to your growth as a writer. Whether you're crafting essays, stories, or articles, the principles of effective paragraph editing will serve as your guiding light.

So, as you venture forth into the vast landscape of writing, approach each blank page with confidence and creativity. Let your words resonate, inspire, and provoke thought. With each paragraph you write, remember your power to shape narratives, influence perspectives, and ignite change.

Embrace the journey of writing with enthusiasm and dedication. Your voice is unique, your stories are valuable, and your potential is boundless. Keep editing, keep writing, and strive to make your mark on the world through the art of the paragraph.

We believe in your ability to captivate, persuade, and enlighten through your writing. So, go forth, dear writers, and let your paragraphs shine brightly as beacons of expression and understanding. The world awaits your words.

APPENDIX

- **Types of Paragraphs and Their Characteristics:**

Paragraph Type	Characteristics
Descriptive	Appeals to senses, vivid imagery
Narrative	Tells a story, chronological sequence
Expository	Presents information, facts, and explanations
Persuasive	Convinces or persuades the reader
Argumentative	Presents a claim with evidence and reasoning

- **Tone of Paragraphs and Their Characteristics:**

Tone	Characteristics
Formal	Polished language, avoids contractions
Informal	Conversational, may use slang or colloquialisms
Serious	Grave or earnest tone, often for weighty topics
Humorous	Amusing or witty, often light-hearted
Persuasive	Assertive, aims to sway opinions

APPENDIX

- **Paragraph Structure and Components:**

Component	Description
Topic Sentence	Main idea or focus of the paragraph
Supporting	Details, examples, evidence that support the topic
Transition	Words or phrases that connect sentences or paragraphs
Sentence	Concluding sentence that summarizes the main idea

- **Common Paragraph Transition Words::**

Transition Word	Function
Furthermore	Adds information or emphasizes a point
However	Indicates contrast or introduces a counterpoint
Therefore	Indicates consequence or conclusion
In addition	Introduces supplementary information
Meanwhile	Indicates simultaneous actions or events

OTHER BOOKS

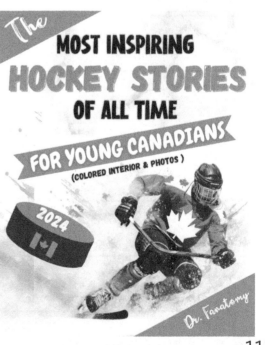

Made in the USA
Coppell, TX
13 November 2024

40145218R00066